MW00387903

GALACTIC SYMBOLS FROM THE 9TH DIMENSION

Gatekeeper Time Codes

KRISTA RAISA

Dedicated to the students of my first online class where they were open

enough to receive a few of these symbols.

Message from the Author:

According to my Mayan Wavespell, I have chosen the path of the Red Spectral Skywalker, or traducere lumina/angelic messenger. In this book, I chose to unlock codes within the Self, to show you a myriad of pathways to Source. The process of writing was, at times, difficult for my logical mind, so you will notice the information-gathering process that took place while creating definitions for each symbol. Between October 2013 and February 2014, I received a set of symbols, each accompanied by a very clear sentence on their meaning, from galactic intelligences.

In this book you will see, that while maintaining focus on a simple task such as meditating on a symbol, your subconscious will relive memories of it's original blueprint. Although our souls are multi-dimensional and ever-expanding, this text will mainly cover information between the third and ninth dimensions of reality, with a greater focus on the latter.

In our present dimension, spiritual people are experiencing "synchronicities" en masse, consuming mono-atomic nutrients by the kilo, and receiving unmentionable downloads of information, similar to the ones in this book. As a channeler I have found some reasons for these things: our brain hemispheres are synchronizing, due to the popularity of world-wide meditations to cure the main illness of Earth: stress/loss of connection to Source. Also, synchronicities unfold through our faster "processing" or de-coding of our downloads. Here is an example of a spiritual "dowload" similar to a moment of déjà vu: monoatomics are the "one atom", also called "Atum" or "completion", as represented by the ending of a major Mayan time-cycle, which is information resonating from the 9th dimension. In this short example, you have been given not only an explanation for a "magical experience", but history through research, as well as intelligent juxtaposition of what skeptics call free association.

Finally, while writing this book, I received information that became increasingly complex as I elaborated on mental projections. One example was after completing symbol #63 and was that of a "Lyran General", a term that unseen galactic intelligences had been referring to for quite some time. I related this to one of the original Angelic Human forms, for which Horemakhet, also known as "The Sphinx", iii

may have been built. Morphemically, a "general" from Lyra may be a genetically + Erran (Pleiadian) + (Al = El =) Elohim, representing it's original form through coding from the constellation of Lyra.

The "main" energy that speaks through this light language is that of *Lyra*, a constellation represented by a harp, responsible for the seeding of most planets in our solar system, also known as Kinich Ahau, to the Mayans, who fully understood time-engineering on Terra-Gaia (Earth). Time-keeping is a process involving the weaving of energies from the 9th dimension via gateways that synchronize with Earth's pulse-rate. This is why the Mayan Calendar was so important- the priest-shamans knew exactly when and where to preform their rites and expand their light-bodies. So, it is my hope that this work will encourage others to look into the Mayan codices, to further decode important dates and locations which improve the quality of our lightwork.

Thank you for being with me on this journey.

Krista Raisa

Sedona, AZ

Introduction

Each symbol comes with direct, channeled terminology, mainly from 9-Dimensional *cosmic* consciousness, more specifically that of Lyran, Andromedan, Pleiadian, Elohim, benevolent Annunaki and Central Sun origin. In this book, you will notice how these consciousness collectives bring in energetics that are not standard English. These groups communicate with their own unique language (using words like "highlighting" to explain a process) and word-order, sometimes leaving out conjunctions and prepositions. The language of the symbols appears as "basic" shapes which are in a specific order, having their own meaning.

The purpose of the symbols is to activate, rebalance, and integrate energy. They are to be used by the initiates, who are ready to feel the energy of each symbol. Individually, they can be written into a longer code, according to your level of integration. They will activate you into writing your own codings and light-writings.

Much like crop-circles, codings are the language of creation and light, implants of remembrance, that will become more active as the vibration of Earth, changes. In addition, the Mayans have left us a very specific "set" of codices, which are beginning to re-awaken in our cellular memory.

As "open'" symbols, you will be able to write inside of them, send power, such as healing energy, or transformation a specific personality program, for instance. Each one will slowly introduce you to a new energy signature, as you activate the mental plane.

In addition to activating symbols on the mental plane (devachanic layer), the ninth dimension will communicate with the very cells of your body, to give you access to the entire dimensional grid -system, as you open yourself to Divine service.

How the Symbols are Transferred

To open a gateway in your heart, to the Higher Teachings of the great Son and the Holy Host *Adonai Tsebayoth*, you must release a certain level of personal will and align with Divine will. This is done through complete humility and belief in Spirit. It is done through a constant communication with the "heart center", even when you feel no one else is listening. *They are always listening.*

After you have deliberately entrusted yourself with the mission to uplift humanity, from a pure space within, you will begin to feel the Light of God, or the One-Mind of Creator/Source/Original Spark. This light contains many codes, which is controlled by Councils of Light, focused in specific star-systems. Individuals will begin contact with these councils and heavens, reaching levels of reality in multiple time streams or "timelines", which are beyond our current perception of time.

The reason we experience time, is because it is the second component to creation, along with light. Have you noticed a certain timelessness when you are completely "in the flow" of your own creation? Have you ever visited certain places where you would say, "the day went by so quickly", or "everything is slow-moving today." This is you, as a Creator god, changing your own time-perception within a light-spectrum. The photonic resonance in your perception, is what keeps your creations moving forward.

As a process, time-keeper codes activate certain gateways within our consciousness. This is fancy terminology for, "you are what you eat." In other words, if you open yourself to an energy spectrum of higher evolutionary teachings, your brain will be fed multiple symbols of color, sound, pictographs, and projections from different realities. Your perceptual readiness will be tested, and your soul will begin to recognize it's own God-Self.

Once the soul recognizes its own "Higher Self", it recognizes the greater part of itself, the "Overself", which it can begin to communicate with (hence the term "Ascension"). When connecting with the Overself, the individuated soul will become aware of the multiple realities its Overself is playing in. With this happening, you may find yourself in another place and time, looking different and learning "extraterrestrial" lessons. You may find yourself teaching on other planes of reality, interacting with other humans in dreamspace, becoming lucid and communicating with beings you have "never" seen before.

It is very human to think that our subconscious is run by programs only. The higher consciousness guiding us knows, at all times, that the influences upon the soul are vast and even beyond the 9th dimension. For the sake of this text, though, we will focus on the layers of reality, which *develop* our consciousness, not box it in!

History of the Earth "suit"

A long time ago, before we were physical human beings, we existed as mainly light and sound, coming directly from Prime Source, or Creator. Over "time", we propelled ourselves through stargates, or dimensional doorways, and created parallel planes of existence, ultimately forming a multi-dimensional reality game. As creators of our own reality programs, we enjoyed moving back and forth between where we came from and where had been, with the Earth game as one of the hardest to circumnavigate. So it is in this reality that we find ourselves unlocking the codes to our existence, in a linear way which will ultimately unite us into the energy of triality (seeing our experience from all "angles" or the angelic perspective), in the Age of Aquarius.

In the earliest times, dating millions and millions of years ago, our energy bodies were more etheric, or more light-body oriented than physically oriented. As these forms would mold into other forms, what we call "shape-shifting", we agreed upon collective experiences to have in the physical. In other words, we decided to have the same physical forms, with variations of course, ultimately searching for the "best" suit. The original suit, however, for the sake of this text, can be referred to as the Angelic Human, or Earth Guardian "suit." It is this program that we are wanting to re-integrate, with the help of these symbols, to trigger ancient cellular memory of what it was like to be a fully-loving, Earth-centered, accelerating being of pure light.

The Nature of the Channelings

Most of the symbols and channeled messages would come through in the evening, where a collective consciousness of "Lyrans" would make their presence known, presenting individual names, each containing a unique energy signature and personality program.

The "essence" is captured in these messages, however, to the skeptic eye, these sentences appear choppy and random. You will see in the following "chant", that the Lyrans were very specific about toning and names, which anchor in their dimensional stream. Here is a direct transcription:

Lyran Chant from "Emsa"

The next verse has been explained by "Emsa", who says that this is from the voice of the Higher Self, which "makes you a 9-Dimensional being." An aspect known as "Emora" says this is Elohim language.

Méi-ahā, Él-a-hā, É-morā, Énō'ós ("That means Enoch help[s] you.")
Éi-a-hā, É-morā, Él-a-hā, Mentō'ór

É-morā, Éi-a-hā, Él-a-hā, Esō'ór

Éi-a-hā, É-morā, Él-a-hā, Esorā

É-morā, É i-a-hā, Él-a- hā, Mmm. (The last sound is the heart frequency sound "A")

Here is the [channeled] transmission that followed:

"Mary...might you know what is holy names for her? Erra make you knowledgeable. Terrans. Erra. Hello. Herra Mekora. Meiaha. Elaha. Erraha. Merraa. Message for you: Great work!"

"Ekora. One of the names is needed. Might you know that name?"

"It is for Highest Energy. Might you know, Meiaha is *Erra*. Erra make you taller. We talking about the races in that place. The rest of the holy names will show who is who. Mighty beings. We talking about the Errans. They want you to see who they are."

Then I received the thought that "Efora" is a messenger.

"We will talk you with them."

Today, it is my understanding (through my research) that "Errans" are Pleiadians, who are working very closely with our Ascension. Some of these Pleiadians have roots within the Lyra system.

Next, I received a list of more names whom the Lyrans say are "helping me." I feel these beings have tried to introduce themselves during 2012, but as a beginner channel it was difficult to adjust to so many streams.

Here are the names with their message: "Enoch. Mykenos. Erraha. Mykonos. **Emos**. You know Emos. Epf. Effeni. Emio. Me, me, me. You know me. Dorians. Emora. Mykenos." (These felt like names from past lives as during 2012 my channel kept referring to people in Sedona as "Dorians", which is a name for ancient Greeks. Also, the name I was given personally was "Emora", which feels like a cosmic aspect, wanting to come through.)

Dimensional Creation

Throughout our cosmic history, we have attempted to define the non-physical dimensions with the help of the greatest psychics, healers and students of the occult. With our linear perception, we have numbered the dimensions we have actual information about and given them specific attributes. Each number, in essence, represents either form or content. With respect to all genders as one, we can still imagine them numerically as containing either Divine "masculine" or Divine "feminine" energy, in other words, the dimensions represent active creation and then defined structure.

When we move from the etheric layer closest to our physical bodies, into the 9th dimension, we pass through several qualities of the soul. These qualities form etheric "templates", or instructions in the form of subatomic particles, also known as the "Divine blueprint." Others would describe these qualities as layers of the aura, for which we typically understand the basic seven. This is why we have so many groups of seven: the seven rays (not discounting the higher rays of creation), the seven sister (Pleiades), the seventh heaven, the seven chakras, the seven seas, the seven earth seals and so on. Currently, we are integrating the higher levels in our Ascension work at this time which has been predicted to continue up to the 9th dimension until 2017-2023 A.D.

Here is an image to describe how we create dimensionally.

Here are Creation [as a process] images, downloaded from the High Council of Orion; 8th and 9th dimensional input:

From left to right (higher to lower) you have:

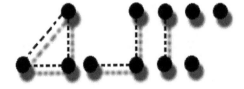

A.Creation as a moving, interdimensional sequence; B. Creation as an interdimensional sequence only; C. Creation as the viewpoint of the sequence, a "junction"; D. Creation as a sequence of focal points or harmony "12 12"; E. Creation as a focal point, such as a number series "1234"

9-Dimensional Leadership

The 9th dimension has been said to link with the Time-Keeper, Tzolkin, on the same octave as galactic codings, the cosmic rays, the Cosmic Heart, and the Cosmic Avatar level. Like Tzolkin, the energy known as El Ra is also a time-keeper, the latter whom I have channeled. Names are important, as Tzolkin is Mayan for "day count" and Ra=the sun, El=Elohim, specifically energized in Alcyone (The Pleiades, where time-records are kept). In short, the 9th dimension is a re-integration process where the kin, or "solar days" are noted so that human priests and Keepers of Time, know when and where to perform specific rituals. What is happening here, with this demonstration of leadership, is a mapping of who-we-truly-are, with hints to spark the subconscious.

As we integrate 9-D energies, the Lyrans have very clearly stated to me, that we must focus on our leadership. To some, leadership may sound like taking command, but this is essentially what the 9th dimension represents. If you can imagine a spiraling galaxy with a vertical axis in the middle [see symbols 49-50], you can mentally re-create an image of leadership commands, coming from a central hub, or pulse-point in the center of the spiral. The Orion Council has explained, that this is also where a lot of inter-dimensional travel takes place, in the eye of the needle, so to speak.

When we travel through these spirals, or "Ascend", we open gateways via the chakras, and travel through hyper levels of the aura. These are levels of light and sound that cannot necessarily be comprehended fully at this time by our human perception, *the 9-D fields are multi-layer and co-exist simultaneously, beyond time and space.* What we **can** comprehend is the knowledge of when the Great Central Sun, a.k.a. Alcyone, the Records of Ra, or "ring" (the level of vibration you have integrated with your Collective) of Christ Consciousness (in the non-religious sense) emits frequencies in the forms of particles, waves and light. These energy transmissions are aligned to the core of our Earth, and are often interpreted as an etheric hum, physical sensation that vibrates our entire system, or an "aha" moment of understanding a telepathic transmission, amongst many other symptoms of Ascension.

When we activate the 9-Dimensional chakras, we communicate with stellar gateways, thus receiving specific points on the grid, I.E., stars that align to specific Earth locations, sounds that harmonize with certain animal, plant and mineral species on our planet, and protocol which propels us into intuitive leadership. In the years to come, many will receive powerful group meditations and lead people into the new era of peace and harmonious communication with all of creation.

On the following pages, you may notice shifts in your vibration: emotional purges, excitement, or a release of your own personal coding. For instance, when students of the "9-Dimensional Leadership Course" were shown a few of the symbols, many began to communicate with their Higher Self aspects and created their own, unique star-language with very specific downloads of knowledge. As the classmates shared their downloads on the Internet, some were so inspired that they began to teach their own classes on their symbols, and created multi-purpose mandalas for the service work.

It is my hope that as you view these symbols, something will re-awaken inside of you. To assist in the process, the descriptions of the symbols have been written in an order that describes how the dimensions operate, instructs you as per their use, and aligns you with a powerful current that is wanting and needing to be recognized.

It is advised that this book be read from start to finish, with breaks in between, as a new energy unfolds through you, onto our beautiful Earth.

1. Andromeda – activate

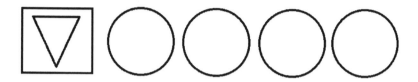

"Takes you to another galaxy."

This first symbol energetically takes us to Andromeda, an energetic "high flow" system of compulsory rates, or specific frequency patterns of energy consciousness. The pulse rate can be imagined like an electrocardiogram. In Andromeda, the patterns are different than they are on Earth. On Earth, the **heart** -rate or **hertz**, is 7.83 HZ. These heartbeats are the pulsewaves that emanate from the iron core of Earth, in specific locations of Earth, which science calls "hot spots."

Andromeda galaxy has a faster heart-rate than Earth and this symbol aligns you to that pulse.

To use the symbol, you can focus it on your heart and imagine a gold light around your auric field. This will transport you into a different consciousness.

2. Andromeda - rebalance

"One. Aligns you to the frequency of one."
"Andromedan intelligence."

This symbol, when placed upon the crown chakra, aligns you to the 9th dimensional Andromedans working with you.

This symbol helps with peace-keeping duties that the Andromedan authorities have.

When you spin the symbol sideways, so that it forms an "x" and then a "+", looped over and over, it begins to expand your Merkabah, or your light vehicle. Doing this kind of work makes you brighter and more visible to the Master scientists who work with and understand these symbols. The point of spinning this symbol is to align you with Galactic Masters, as it increases the vibration of your lightbody.

3. Andromeda – reintegrate

"Andromedan intelligence."
"Andromedan 8-D beings."

The frequency of this symbol represents the hierarchy structure of 8-D, which is needed when we work with 9-D. This is from being who work in the "executive branch" of the system, where spiritual laws are made in light-form. You can see this as the layer where inpired codings from 9-D enter in light-form to weave a fabric of creation. So, whereas 9-D writes program codes, the 8-D beings structure it as the free-flowing energy is given purpose and laws.

To use this symbol it is best to write it on a piece of paper with the intention of contacting this energy. You may write a series similar to "binary" code, which are actually input codes that align to a specific Mayan Codex.

4. Andromeda – rebalance, restructure, awaken

"For helping with 9-Dimensional energies."

All dimensions are joined together by a dimension which behaves as an axis. Therefore, it only makes sense that 8th and 9th dimensional energies co-operate.

The first symbol in this set means "in accordance with Divine Timing." The circle indicates a cycle of completion, the triangle, a unity, and the final square is timelessness. In other words, when a sequence ends in a square, it means it is open to continue.

To use this symbol, it is best to write it on a piece of paper and continue the sequence according to your Higher Self's instructions.

5. Andromeda – awaken, align, restructure, rebalance, unity

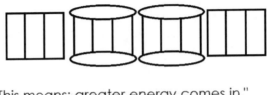

"This means: greater energy comes in."

 =symbol for 9D energy

Many *different* symbols are used for anchoring the energy of the 9th Dimension. This is one of many. It shows the parallel dimensions in one sequence. When you write 9D symbols in a sequence, it pairs dimensions and activates the subconscious.

These help to correct the time-field polarization. Techniques that allow us to integrate "Who We Truly Are" include the integration of time-field symbols from the Meta-Galactic core.

6. Andromeda – Meta-Galactic core -attunement symbol

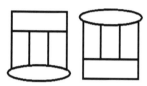

"This means: adjustment phase, 9-Dimensional alignment, corrections being made."

Many of these symbols are made for energetic adjustments, and are recognized by the subconscious, *not* the ego.

Also, the names you will read of in this book, mostly begin with the letter "E" and these four names were given after I drew these 6 symbols: "ENYA, ELIYA, ENLA, ENDRA." The Lyrans said these are "names for great beings of Andromeda."

Again, these symbols are best used when written onto a peace of paper and used in mediation. They are simple symbols which active time-codes.

7. Alcyone – activate, awaken, realign

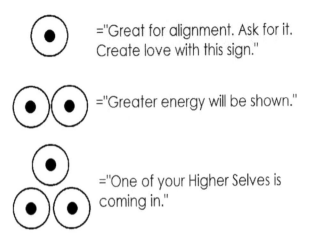

="Great for alignment. Ask for it. Create love with this sign."

="Greater energy will be shown."

="One of your Higher Selves is coming in."

Most of the symbols are spherical, although there are several instances where three lines occur, as with Mayan numbers.

In Alcyone, the Library which stores all the records of the constellation are gifted more information when beings come and enter the Library. This symbol will help you to remember information from the library: past-lives, future lives, and present moment "understandings." They like to gather information in though-form, and so to "store" thought-form energy, a crystalline database must be used to program the specific frequencies of timelines, into a unified, cohesive-etheric form.

8. Lyra – wave structures

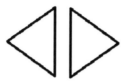

"Transmission Recording"

Although simple, through this book, you receive the frequencies.It was not specified how this transmission was being recorded, however, the transmission is the actual "downloading" and drawing of this symbol. This works with energy waves, as opposed to energy particles.

It is assumed that when drawing this symbol, you consciously download information into it, while other symbols are for retreiving information. To the human mind, this represents the triangular structure that makes up our crystals and the pyramidal structures that make up our human brain. The collective energy known as "Mary" describes this symbol as: A two-way focal point.

9. Lyra - Genetics Formatting, activator

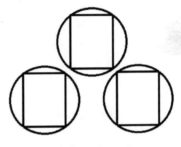

Training Device

The Orion Council has presented a "Training Officer" several times in *Orion Council, Here* (2013). It is the base of the planet design training program of Antareans, who are sisters of Arcturians. The Antareans have mastered planet design. These symbols relate to energy-training. Energy-training takes place in several sectors of the Orion constellation, relating to Earth. This device in particular corresponds to frequency codes and mind "opening", in the galactic ambassadors on Earth. Some specific frequencies in the device include: organic material -reorganization, time-fusion, elemental reconstruction mechanisms and galactic "ambassadorship" coding. Consider them instructional and relating to one's purpose. The programming of major devices such as this comes from Lyra consciousness.

Many of the extraterrestrial machines are said to use "organic" materials, as opposed to inorganic materials, since the time-codes in organic material (non-influenced by humanoid intelligences) are more *relatable* to their purpose. When time-codes are activated with a machine, the propulsion rate must link to the original sequence of the coding. Anything that has been misused, has, indeed, done a kind of reverse-engineering which does not suit the original "structure". There is spiritual terminology for this structure, which I can only describe as "God's plan."

10. Lyra - "Coding purpose"

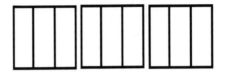

Organic Machinery

This is a reconstructing mechanism for the mind-body-spirit construct, as it becomes inter-stellar and participates in time-travel. The dimensional fields begin to open when one expands via "organic starship." The purpose of this symbol is "time-coding" where the time-field changes at a rapid rate, or accelerated frequency. What this means it that the future codings of Earth people will contain a reconstructed organic constituent, and machinery is not metals, it is actually the *programing* of our brains which allows for this expansion to occur into new thinking methods.

This code does not need to be written, the explanation is enough to trigger cellular memory.

13

11a.,11b. & 12. Andromeda & Pleiades - Attunement

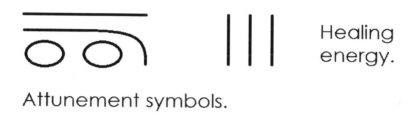

Healing energy.

Attunement symbols.

These symbols were channeled for a client, so the curvy lines are very unique to the symbols in this entire book. I have noticed that "elven" writing has more curvature than other symbols, however, you can see that the second symbol is one that is unique to Andromeda and also is a sideways version of the Mayan number for 15.

"44 Angels here with this symbol."

14

Symbol 11b has to do with the light-body, according to the Elohim.

Symbol 12 is a Pleiadian-Andromedan symbol for calling in angels

and activating the light-body.

13. - 16. Elohim - Pleiades - Attunement

Here is a sign for giving light to people.

Here is the top of a spiral. It says you are a messenger of God.

Greater frequency alignment.

This is for heightening your senses (e.g. third eye)

The triangle "download" was received in the winter of 2012, and are referred to as "Pleiadian Healing Triangles." Also, the concentric circles, I later discovered, appeared in my videos and other lightworkers had begun to see them. These, apparently, are spiraling vortices viewed from above, also representing portals to other dimensions. This symbol is used to bring beings in and out of dimensions and should be done with the greatest caution.

"All particles of light align with this one", say the Elohim, in reference to the 4-lined symbol for "greater frequency alignment." There exists a sphere of consciousness deep within us, which we can access or activate upon will. When this begins to spin it creates light-waves, or lines, that are paralleled. These lines are like "light-weaving", and this is how we integrate the interdimensional symbols' frequencies. Inside of the sphere of consciousness, are all original programs. The sphere is located on the right side of the brain.

Many of these symbols can be written in an arc, or a circle, as the placement of the symbols creates a unification which contains its own energy form.

The collective "Mary" comments on symbol 14: two Elohim signs inside of a circle.

17.-20. "Pleiadian Healing Triangles"

Manifestation triangle.

Frequency generator.

Great beings come in with this.

Use for Attunement.

I received the guidance for manifestation as follows: "Draw your desires into a triangle, write down names of deities or power-beings to increase the potency of [the] request."

Basically, the triangle will amplify any symbol you write.

Each triangle within a circle is to be used by writing affirmations or the names of beings or energies, that you wish to work with. The triangle amplifies their energy and the circle contains the energy. When written on paper, "they" say everything is amplified. As with all the symbols, intent is everything.

Finally you may notice these on insignias and on areas like the forehead. It is my understanding that they will telepathically send you mental healing images through the third eye, which is why many of us believe they have the triangles physically on their foreheads.

21. Lyran-**Andromedan** "resonance" symbol #1

For the next symbol I received the command: "Make a 9-Dimensional Language -sign. Then write your name."

Your name

"They" said: "Now, that is a 9-Dimensional sign. It means writing-talk. There was light coming indirectly from the sign. Tell your 9-Dimensional Higher Self to align with this sign. Now, write your name indirectly with this sign. This aligns you to that creative aspect in the 9th Dimension."

The odd-numbered dimensions are more creative in essence, and even-numbered dimensions give form and structure to the creative, odd dimensions. When 9-dimensional energy is manifested, the 8th dimension becomes a conduit of that energy and mirrors it into the 6th dimension where the geometry is manifested.

22. Lyran-**Andromedan** resonance symbol #2

The next command was: "Now, write a self-aligning word. It is for [your] leadership role to be activated. With that, indirectly write your name."

Your name

"They" explained for this one: "Now that means All are aligned [...] That is good. We think you are doing very well."

The next six symbols were co-written with "Emsa", who helped attune me to the 9th Dimension. "They" told me: "Take time, for these will be enormously powerful." If you at all feel strange, "they" say to first "empty yourself" before receiving these symbols, which accumulate the Divine Essence." For several weeks, after drawing this symbol, the Lyrans have been guiding me to practice "emptiness."

With this symbol we also learn to think outside of the box. For instance, "your name" may also mean "your name for a grid location/Mayan calendar sate." We *must* remember that this is "alien" language and not standard English.

23. Lyran-**Andromedan** Intelligence

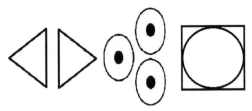

This is for advancement of
the species.

As you can see, these are the symbols for "recording, alignment" and "training device", written in one stream. The energies are those of the Elohim, Lyra, Andromeda and the Pleiades, combined into one, written language. Perhaps this is a signal that the purpose of some humans is to document or "record" their reality, then somehow align their energies to Spirit, as a part of their *training*, although this is a very simple translation of the sentence. If one can imagine the "codes" of our genetics combining, perhaps this combination of languages is reflecting that there are many super-races existing, with strains from different star systems.

23

24, 25. Andromedan writing for "Source Code"

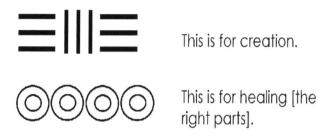

This is for creation.

This is for healing [the right parts].

Previously, in symbol 21, we see the semi-circles. These are showing the organization of particles and how duality "splits" its consciousness. You will see the semi-circles in later symbols.

Here is what they say about symbol 24: "Inside of the lines there arrows. Message is, train yourself to highlight, and the arrows will become clear. Mary comes in with this symbol."

For the circles in these symbols [25] you have multiples of unification. If you can imagine these circles as cycles of creation, co-operating simultaneously, yet individually evolving, you will understand the duality principle of the semi-circles. On the other hand, the straight lines [24] represent form, concepts, singularities and *separation* within groups of consciousness. For whenever we create, we must individuate ourselves from the whole, although in time, we must re-unify with the Source, and blend back into wholeness, which is represented by the "healing" circles.

When written in sequence, you have masculine creation with feminine intuition, and so the rotation between the straight and curvy symbols, is what makes Source Code.

In addition, if you were to fill in the circle in the middle of the larger circles, you would have a more focused energy. This moves us into Pleiadian training, as much of the energy training in the Pleiades comes from Andromeda. In other words, what they have told me, is that a lot of the Andromedan energy helps prepare us for the Pleiadian "language" of the light. These are to ease you into the triangles that the Pleiadians "write" with.

The training described by the Andromedans, is the preparation for light-beings to become Pleiadian Messengers. Most of the Messengers incarnated, now, are people who should be working with the Peace symbols, as they have trained to be ambassadors of Peace. They have many Pleiadian contacts and are encouraged to work with their groups, which are situated around the globe. The Lyrans have told me that they are already forming groups around the world, which most of us call "Starseeds."

In the next set of Pleiadian symbols, you will see these are "keys", and when you have keys to consciousness, it unlocks or triggers cellular-level coding that is only understood by the subconscious.

26-30. Messenger symbols from the Pleiades – Light codons, particle assimilation

This is for anointing (special sign, tracing back to many beings).

This is for Higher Self becoming evenly aligned.

This is for sound frequency to be heard from different energy pathway to the current.

This is for the accumulation of light particles.

The frequencies of the symbols are patience [26], acceleration [27], readiness/evening out/balancing our your energy levels [28], intuition [29] and guidance [30]. In 27, the black triangle signals energy moving upwards. It is a very powerful "Ascension symbol." The magnetics involved in all symbols is represented by the empty triangle, but when it is a solid color, it represents polarities being "released", which is also the process of Ascension. The empty triangle (on the left side of 27) has been described by the energy of "Aten" as: "deliberate work by descent."

Next, they said, "Now this is interesting. This is how the creation of your name happens, with two parts of your name. It will attune you to the energy of your name." And they asked that I write my name and draw three lines in between my name, which is "KRISTA" and has six letters. Next they wanted me to draw a figure-eight around my name, encircling the "KRI" and the "STA" separately.

My thought was that the second form looked like two cells splitting into duality.

On the other hand, as with the dimensions, one can separate the "masculine" from the "feminine" in the forms of consonants and vowel-sounds, and re-write ones name according to an original language form, resembling ancient Hermetic, Khemetic, Hebrew, Japanese or Hawaiian phonotactics. So, "Krista" becomes KA – RE – SU – TA, where the morphemes explain some of the soul's mission.

Language decoding of "KRISTA" example:

KA = vital force or soul

RE/RI = the sun

SA/SU = wisdom

TA = world/land/Earth, originating from Ptah, the Neter/Creator god/Elohim

Let us break down my mother's name, "KATHERINE":

KA/Kha = vital force or soul
TA = above
HE = from YHWH "Yod He Vod He", also Water, Binah, Memory, Grail, the number five
RE/RI = the sun
NU = "watery one", the mother, the beginning of everything

Here we see the beginnings of how original sound became cellular duality, and finally *concepts*.

31-40. Resonance symbols

The next set of symbols resembles more of a language of "tones."

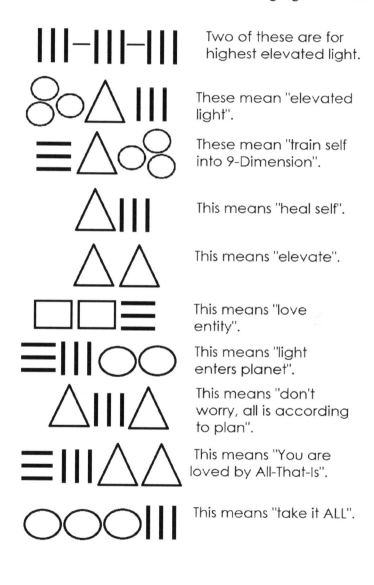

Two of these are for highest elevated light.

These mean "elevated light".

These mean "train self into 9-Dimension".

This means "heal self".

This means "elevate".

This means "love entity".

This means "light enters planet".

This means "don't worry, all is according to plan".

This means "You are loved by All-That-Is".

This means "take it ALL".

"A lot of it's from Directive", they said. And I asked, "What am I supposed to do?" They said, "Direct energy."

Similar to the Pleiadian attunement signs, when you write these in a circle, they create a moving geometry in the 6th dimension. As you imagine the symbol, it can be seen etherically. Triangles, when formed in a circle, are especially powerful. Many of the Lyrans use this sort of geometry for medtation.

The circle inside of the triangle increases the resonance factor and there is a sort of energetic stimulation that takes place. Whenever a symbol is placed upon another symbol, you have greater energy, but one must be careful when creating combinations, as they truly form in the ethers with energy of their own.

41. Central Sun Frequency Adjustor

For aligning you with the lightbody.

The circle in this image also represents the "sun disk", which the Lyrans frequently refer to as "Aten." There are many groups of Lyrans and not all use this symbol to refer to the Central Sun. The Central Sun, they say, has infinite form, and the group here, says the circle describes it best, as it is the unification of the One, the All.

This adjustment occurs as you propel the parallel lines around the circle in a clock-wise motion. You can imagine it spinning like a shot-put thrower at the Olympics. When this begins to spin, it creates etheric "sparks" which show how Source creates unto itself.

They say this sign is for "remembering Creation."

42a, 42b, 43. Seraphim – Elohim Signs

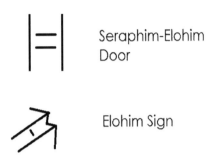

Seraphim-Elohim
Door

Elohim Sign

These light symbols have to do with the 9th dimension, the frequency of Mary, and the Lyrans. The Collective consciousness known as "Mary" works very closely with the Seraphim angels. The next message for me was: "Train yourself to write the language of light" and I received the command to create a "9-Dimensional Seraphim-Elohim Door" as well as a "9-D Elohim sign."

Dimensional
Doorway being shut

44-50. Interdimensional weaving process

The next series of symbols were very interesting. The symbol for "going into dimensions" looks very similar to a milky way black hole, which can emit incredible X-rays that are equivalent to the energy of the sun if not more. After writing these they said, "Now, we know you are wondering why, but see it as a task/completion/rules for awakening. Might we know, you are writing light-language."

= 9 Dimension

9

Some refer to the pineal gland as the "Eye of Ra", also, "the seat of the soul", basically where the magic takes place. This is the "all-seeing" master third eye, which humanity is currently decalcifying. When this is fully active we will have clear light-language communication, and interdimensional access for more knowledge.

=Acceleration of
pineal gland into the
9th Dimension

-> Pineal gland
(Has access codes
to Dimensions)

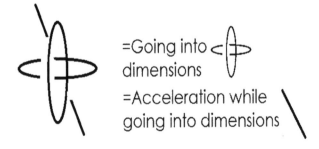

=Going into
dimensions

=Acceleration while
going into dimensions

=Reaches a
higher platform

As you can see, a line is drawn upwards from the 9th dimension, and in the next symbol you can see several more until you hit what may be the 12th dimension.

The overlapping ovals represent an interesting message from the Lyrans, which was that our Earth actually has four poles, instead of two. These could be inter-dimensional poles, as the Orion Council suggested that the "inner Earth" is simply a reflection reality of what we currently experience on the surface.

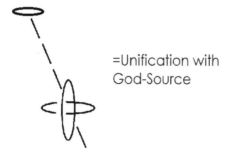

=Unification with
God-Source

After completing all the symbols, I see that, indeed, these have been written in a very important sequence. The following symbols may actually be a close-up of the pineal gland, and a simplified explanation of how it works. So, long story short, as above, so below.

[Image of spiraling galaxy with an axis point, to help define the concept of the 9th dimension, which acts as a link to the other dimensions.]

51-54. How to Heal Consciousness Separation

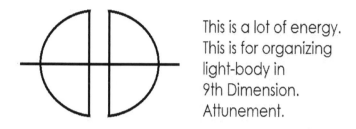

This is a lot of energy.
This is for organizing
light-body in
9th Dimension.
Attunement.

Next, they gave the command: "Now draw. Heal with this sign." I focused the energy of healing while drawing this, which reminds me of the left and right hemispheres of the brain, and how they need to work together, not independently of one another, which applies to people also.

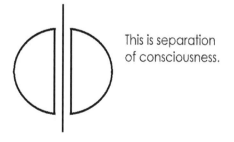

This is separation
of consciousness.

38

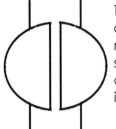

This is consciousness separation also, but isn't for the whole. It means, consciousness can be separate but if it is held in doubt/fear it will not remember it is part of the whole.

These symbols must be spun counter-clockwise to stimulate subconscious memory of particle assimilation. What this means, is that the Elohim gateway opens, when you stimulate the pineal through a mental visualization.

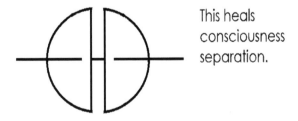

This heals consciousness separation.

As you can see, the lines appear to strike through the symbol, which would give it 3-dimensionality.

This is particle assimilation. Each aspect of the Whole begins to unite out of separation.

55. Unknown

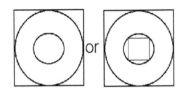 This is for continuity of the species.

After you have healed consciousness separation, you can begin to imagine the Merkabah inside of a multi-layer box. The Lyrans had been showing me "boxes" for several weeks and I did not realize what they were while giving readings to people.

Each box is where creation happens. The angles show that you are in a specific dimension. If you were to only exist within a circle, you would have endless creation. The boxes actually give form to the circle, which represents the "even-numbered" dimensions, such as 4,6, and 8. The box would represent dimensions 5, 7 and 9. When you get to dimension #11, you enter through an Elohim door, and go through "particle assimilation." As you can now see, each symbol also represents a process our consciousness goes through when we invest in inter-stellar travel, through the dimensions.

56. Pleiades – Ascension

 This is for Enlightenment.

"Mary comes in with this symbol."

To some, the energy of Mary has been attributed to the energy of the Christ, however, this symbol may look like a simple subconscious program we have of Star Beings, or, the natural elements of the Earth. Next, they said: "The rays of light, work on the sign that you make." The term "rays" refers to light-signatures which have been given to Master collectives, each representing or uniting under the agreement of a unique area of expertise, such as harmony, balance, healing or music. These are also represented by what many of us know as the "virtue" Angels in Christianity.

57. Pleiades – Bermuda Triangle Gateway Opening

 This is for Peace and Unity.

In the 5th dimension and beyond, we begin to work as collectives, or "containers" of energy. The Ascension of our Earth has been described to me as collectives beside collectives, or circles among circles, each a grouping of light-workers with their own unique qualities. Some humans and Lyrans alike, feel that during Ascension, we will group into smaller communities with a similar vision, anchoring the inner teachings of Oneness.

This symbol seems to be a Pleiadian depiction of the group energy of Ascension or Enlightenment, contained in a healing circle, as they have added the qualities of peace and unity to this symbol.

At the moment, this symbol will link you to planetary work on the Bermuda Triangle.

58. Pleiadian Healing Triangle

Healing Triangle.

This was one of the first symbols I received from galactic consciousness. It was sent directly into the third eye and felt as if it would work well when a quartz "generator" crystal was placed upon it. Again, this works as a manifestation symbol, because the circle requires that one place their intention or harmonious words into the circle. As in ceremonial magic, you can add names of deities you work with or celestial beings to call them in with this sign. The circle contains the energy, which is then amplified by the triangle, which is similar to the way orgonite works: you have organic material (crystals) attracting energy into inorganic material (such as resin), which is then amplified by a third component (metal). As with a crystal, the triangle has "points" which sent energy outwards from the center. It is therefore no wonder that this symbol and similar ones have been used throughout human history. The Pleiadians, however, use this specifically for healing and balancing the heart-rate.

59. Pleiadian Healing Triangle with Mary's energy

Healing Extra
Components of the Soul.

Here is the transmission that followed: "Central Sun energy particles align with this sign. Several beings come in with this sign. Unification of soul-parts happens with this insignia. Many use these symbols to integrate "allowance", which is universal access to Central Sun energetics. Message is to hold onto the place within one's self, and unify with All-That-Is."

60. Pleiades - "Aggregate"

This is Expansion.

When units of consciousness are placed within a triangle, as within our brains, we have an alignment (such as the brain hemispheres). The channeled aspect, known as Emora, is writing in a way that specifies each symbol according to their dialectic frequency pattern, in Lyran communication (symbolic frequencies). She is showing us that when we align both hemispheres of our brain, we begin to accelerate, which creates a rotation speed, thus generating a wider expansion.

Each triangle is represented by a square, an on-going movement, containing a triad of creation and communication. As we place our consciousness within a triangle, each begins to revolve and affect the mirroring of the next symbol.

61. Lyra

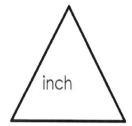 This is for delegating matters of Spiritual Concepts (A triangle with a unit of measurement inside it).

They gave the command: "Now draw a unit of measurement." I drew an inch. […] "Now draw another line, in the middle, dissecting it. […] There are two components, here. One is a unit of measurement. The other is a species replica."

Lyrans are very much focused on creating life, as many took part in this Earth experiment long ago. Therefore, it would make sense that they use a symbol for "replicating" species, as I have found through the channelings that many E.T. intelligences are primarily focused on their "jobs", which include: collecting samples (a Pleiadian came through, once, that was very excited about collecting wood chips with life-forms on it); maintaining life on their ships; beaming themselves in their light-bodies onto Earth, and then materializing and re-materializing into physical form.

Purpose: making sure intervals occur so that making life is harmonious.

62. Lyra – Intuitive Development; Hatshepsut

This means intuition acceleration/ intuition mapping/ precognitive skills and higher level intelligence.

Several of the Lyran energies come in with group collectives, which refer to ancient names like Menkaure (the pharaoh and 3rd great pyramid), "Aten" (the solar disk), "Helios" (the solar logos), and introduce themselves, e.g. "We are the Horus Collective." A consciousness referring to "Hatshepsut" specifically works with this symbol.

Names are most likely used, that would be known to myself, the channel, and therefore are not subject to being politically correct, as the greatest importance is within the energy signature of the communication. The beings say this is a "relationsl perspective."

During the time of Hatshepsut, Abraham was also present upon Earth, which may be why the famous channel known as "Esther Hicks" is channeling that very group consciousness. We are basically re-working

timelines of 144,000 kin or days, which make up what the Mayans call

a "Baktun."

To use this symbol, request that you integrate the Hatshepsut

"timeline" and notice a golden light which enters the pineal gland and

illuminates the receiving end of your body.

63. Lyra – Pleiades – Alcyone – Record-Keeper Symbol

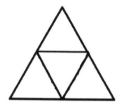 Evolution - Creation -
Acceleration -
Knowledge - Healing -
Knowing - Faster
Vibration

The intricacies of this symbol are evident- it imbues several unique qualities.

"The gestation period involved in the integration of this sign is tenfold. It's unique qualities stem from the Higher Self, elevated *aspect*, which, in retrospect, is triangular. Once the rotational angles of the triangles each start spinning, the inner triangle clock-wise and the outer triangle counter-clockwise, the head begins to form a mass. In other words, the angles represent the unison, or synchronization of the left and right hemispheres, while the combination of particles generated from the rotation create a mass around the brain.

Tenfold is the increase of the [Human-Mind brain] field, as if the Fibonacci/Vitruvian Man were spiraling inside of a pentagonal device."

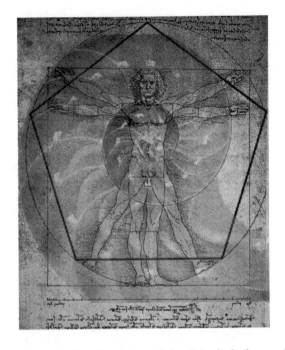

Here, we are seeing the beginnings of the Merkabah, or the *vehicle* of Man, which the Lyrans refer to as the "training device." What they mean is the *actual human body*, coded by the light-language of the Elohim as guided by Prime Creator. We are Source-Code in itself!

In relation to the Golden Spiral, as represented by the opaque, nautilus shell, the "tenfold energy" is the makeup of the Divine Blueprint. In this primal matrix code, interconnected grids are spiraling out of one grand template. You can see with the two triangles, triplets beginning the formation of grids, or to take it to the next level, DNA codons. Importantly, the merkabah is what is used to travel inter-dimensionally, coordinating with the Ascended Masters, taking on any form that is needed to experience creation. The Hosts, as communicated through Orion, use the Merkabah to deliver messages of the Great Plan, which we can interpret (receiving into the right brain hemisphere and translated by the left) when aligned to our Higher Selves in the 5th dimension. Furthermore, when we align with the Solar Logoi known as "Helios" or the Galactic Logos known as "Melchior", we ignite the fire-letters within and begin translation of the 9-D emanations, translated into light from the monads within the 8th dimension, through the geo-translation devices held within the 6th. This is where the interpenetration of the Merkabic vehicles occur, as collectives of consciousness transmit frequencies from the Universal mind.

54

64.-67. Lyra – Pleiades – Maya Timex, Gatekeeper codes

With this symbol they gave the command: "Now, draw a line around the circle. You can write anything in that space. We write your name in that space. […] Align with the 9-D Lyran energies and put your name in that space. […] We [are] talking about the frequency of the 9th Dimension. […] Take time with people...healing forces you are working with. […] You will take a minute, now. That is all. Thank you."

The next message went like this: "Mary energy [is] coming in with your writing. Creative energies. Creation makes All things. Creation is everything. Might you know who you are? Creation is love. Creation is greatness. Create light. Indirectly work with yourself. Forces come in to help you. Forces of love. We will tell you more, soon. We love you. Thank you."

Later on, I received another message: "Now we will write the coding for the Lyran Energies. 111 222 333 444. We are writing in Lyran Language. Council of Elders. Now we send you 9-Dimensional Light-writing. Writing your name with this language connects you to the 9-D Lyran energy."

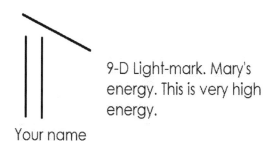

9-D Light-mark. Mary's energy. This is very high energy.

Your name

They said, "Great work!"

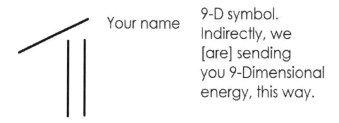

Your name

9-D symbol. Indirectly, we [are] sending you 9-Dimensional energy, this way.

"Now, great work. We want you to write another symbol."

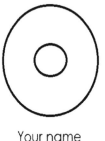

You [are] releasing with [this] symbol.

Your name

Several of these timex codes are related to the *inspiration* of the soul. Each symbol contains its own "healing" property, you could say, given a specific task (which is a complete understatement). The frequencies emanating from each symbol is immense.

When our mind-chatter ends, we will notice that a simple exercise can magnify our entire subconscious routine.

The second and third symbols in this series of four, are gatekeeper codes, where a slanted mark appears above two vertical lines. Not only do they work with the energy of Mary, but a being named Simeon works alongside them (this name has come through for other modern channels as well, representing energies of the 7th dimension and more). They tell me that writing names with symbols is how hieroglyphics were formed.

68.-69. Lyra

The next symbol refer to "Maest", a name/word which the Lyrans

spelled out for me.

This is for creation in the
Maest.
[This] makes a 9-D
alignment with other
beings. E.g. Mary.

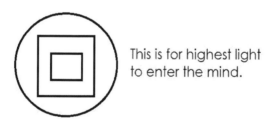

This is for highest light
to enter the mind.

"There will be a shift in your conscious mind when you write these

symbols [Lyran light-writing]." Later, I found that "MEST" stands for

matter – energy – space- time.

58

70-77. Lyra – Creation symbols

The next symbol, they said, is "very close to [the] heart." They also

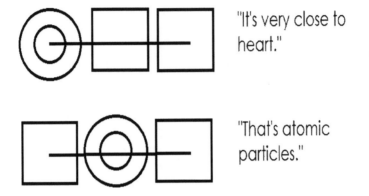

"It's very close to heart."

"That's atomic particles."

said, "There will be another. You send a 9-Dimensional light-writer through your conscious[ness]."[74,75]

Next, they said "There will be too many spheres for you to write simultaneously. Get adjusted, first." I needed to relax in my chair and allow the light-writer to come in.

"These writings are needed because they will help expand consciousness."

Here is an entire sequence:

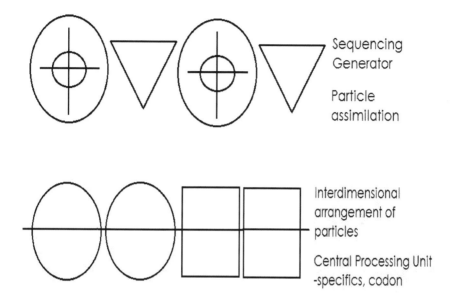

Sequencing
Generator

Particle
assimilation

Interdimensional
arrangement of
particles

Central Processing Unit
-specifics, codon

After writing this symbol, they said: "Elohim were writing words in the Neter."

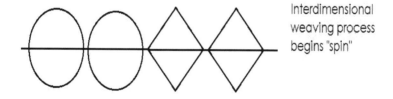

Interdimensional
weaving process
begins "spin"

60

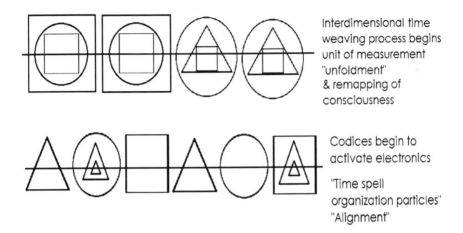

Interdimensional time weaving process begins unit of measurement "unfoldment" & remapping of consciousness

Codices begin to activate electronics

"Time spell organization particles" "Alignment"

After writing this symbol they said "Nineveh", so, it would be wise to integrate any timelines associated with this place or Babylon. Interestingly, Emsa and Orion Council allowed for a message from the Annunaki-Elohim, whom some of the Lyrans refer to as the "destroyer Angels", although this term also refers to higher-ranking angels. They were allowed to share that they hold a belief that "the All must unite under the One", and felt that their destructive nature had to happen for certain processes to unfold on our Earth.

The next symbol is from the Annunaki themselves, which they say opens a gateway for Seraphim to enter certain reality programs, which they have (unfortunately) used for manipulation. However, it is my understanding that the Annunaki communicating have integrated the Oneness program into their soul-matrix.

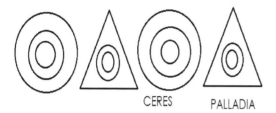

Frequency modulation, 7-7-7

time codex, multiple reality program activate

CERES   PALLADIA

This symbol has placed "names" underneath, which are location names that may give a hint as to how these should be used.

It occurred to me before writing "CERES", that we are currently working with the "Whale Program", which has specific instructions having to do with Sirius B cetaceans. Several of the benevolently integrated Annunaki refer to this program as the "Arc Oleon", and are serving by sharing that the Palisades is a main location for energetically retreiving timex codes from Sirius B (which we can access in meditation).

Next they have shared an entire "download map" for locations that are sending out timex codes in the world. They call these "grid locations", which are really gateways, working with a specific symbol they have given, to amplify the energies of that place and integrate the new Golden matrix.

Benevolent Annunaki - Earth Council grid-points

Major U.S.A. Grid-points:

Sedona, Arizona (also Tempe)

Little Rock, Arkansas (+12 more, including minor points: Cherokee Village; Front Range Mountains; Sherwood)

Pasadena, California (also: Golden Gate National Park; San Diego)

Nederland, Colorado (also: Colorado Springs)

Sarasota Springs, Florida (also: Callaway, Green Acres; Orlando)

Elder, Georgia (minor points: Lake Margaret)

English, Indiana

Topeka, Kansas

Canton, Michigan

Minneapolis, Minnesota

Hernando, Mississippi (minor points: Lambert)

Rosebud, Montana

Las Vegas, Nevada

Point Pleasant, New Jersey

Cincinnati, Ohio

Portland, Oregon

Houston, Texas (minor points: Alamo, Bedford)

Chesapeake Bay, Virginia (also: Pleasant Valley)

Seattle, Washington

Milwaukee, Wisconsin (minor points: Greendale)

Minor U.S.A. Grid-points:

Los Angeles, California

64

New Orleans, Louisiana

Arlington, Massachusetts

Queens, New York

International grid-points [major ones in bold]:

Kingsford, New South Wales, Australia

Greater Sudbury, Ontario, Canada (also: Division No. 17, Saskatchewan)

Guangdong, China (also Nanjing)

Silkeborg, Denmark

*Mount Sinai, Egypt

Montaiguët-en-Forez, France

Soest, Germany

Tblisi, Georgia

Maharashtra, India

Jerusalem, Israel

Perugia, Italy

West Sumatra, Indonesia

Hokkaido, Japan (*airport)

Priekuļu novads, Latvia

Skopje, Macedonia

Penang, Malaysia

North Province, Maldives

Veracruz, Mexico (also: **Mexico City**)

Landgraaf, Netherlands

Calabarzon, Philippines

Warsaw, Poland

*Transylvania/Ardeal, Romania

Malaga, Spain (also Pontevedra)

KwaZulu-Natal, South Africa (also: Cape Town; Gauteng)

Steffisburg, Switzerland

Beyoğlu, Turkey

Cornwall, U.K. (also: **Birmingham**; **Eastchurch**; **Greenwich** [which they call the "capital of the country"] in London; Hartford; Ilford; Killington; Newcastle upon Tyne; **Southend-on-Sea**)

Before publishing with book, I have done private meditations with a friend, in which we would travel to a specific Earth location, enter in "grid codes" (numerical series with light language) and activate certain gateways, to assist our "teams." Sometimes we would travel to space-ships, under water, or into parallel realities. We also feel that we are adjusting timelines, and attempting to manifest the most benevolent ones.

What you can do with these locations, is enter them in meditation and follow your intuition on whatever work needs to be done in this areas. Perhaps you will also notice the recalibration happening automatically, or you will channel your own locations.

I see these locations as having spiraling vortices of energy, upon which we can place the correct symbol (similar to crop-circles). Also, each location will activate a gate, which is literally in a specific star or star system.

In the past, these rituals were performed by anointed priests, but in this lifetime, the information is coming through cellular or subconscious memory recall, with specific people who are continually awakening to their own legacies.

78a, 78b. Lyra – Genetics formattor

These were the instructions for this symbol:

"First draw a circle. Then draw a line going up and down, in the middle of the circle. If you were to write your name in the middle of the circle, we would send you light (directly). Then draw two circles on the right side of the line. These would align your higher aspect for

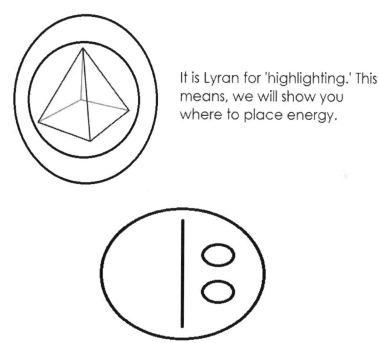

It is Lyran for 'highlighting.' This means, we will show you where to place energy.

highlighting."

Highlighting means, making it known that now, certain choices have

68

to be made, while we see the widening gap between negative and positive polarities.

The instructions continue: "Inside of the circles are also two smaller squares (not depicted here). The top square would rotate clock-wise and the bottom would rotate counter-clockwise. The "spindles" (genetic formatting units) create "wires" (as in wiring), a process which determines our Ascension symptoms. Sometimes the "spindles" go hangwire and we have headaches or stomache aches. This is not the intention of this symbol. It should be known that once you activate your cellular memory, through recall, practice and achieving a high level of light, the processes which your body is involved in, are no longer the same.

Sometimes we act upon will, and change the formats of these minute parts of ourselves, yet, there will always be an evolution of consciousness regardless. It is *you*, who determines the velocity at which you accelerate *yourself*.

The Consciousness Programming of Earth is at the moment (in 2014) is "manifest tenfold." In 12 years is should have accelerated by twenty. This means, faster accumulation(s) of knowledge, further studies in esoterics developed, alleviation of Earth "symptoms" and channeled guidance from star beings. We know, that once we unite under the Sun (Aten), we will accelerate the Mass Consciousness Program. It is up to us, to complete our missions (in a timely fashion). Twice, you have been to the Central Sun, and you will go back."

79. Lyra & Central Sun Beings – Love of God (symbol)

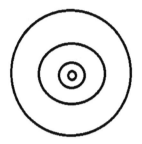

Lyra loves (the)
peace and so we
write the symbol for it.
Love-symbol.

Message:

"Here, we see a symbol which the channel has noticed in several of her videos, on the wall, in her home, everywhere. She was convinced it was for Ascension Gateways, for which she is partially correct. Inside of the first larger circle, are the accumulated particles which God Source has sent to you, personally. We understand this as the masses awaken to their Sovereignty. Once you claim your Sovereignty, you will notice the circles appearing. This is a Source Code to guide you when you are not aware of the assistance you have been given. At all time, we watch. We are Central Sun beings. We are ALL in the center of the circle. You are experiencing distance from the center. This was supposed to happen. It is."

When our non-physical friends talk about the "Central Sun", it is my understanding that they are referring to a vast energy that encompasses our entire solar system. They tell me the name, "Kinich Ahau", which came to me **two years after** channeling the word "Helios" on repeat (Kinich Ahau, the Mayan Light-Keeper God, also known as Helios), alongside "Horus", "Hatshepsut", "Dorians", and words like "Duat."

I feel that we are given pieces of the puzzle to work our way back to the original love that so created us.

The reason for connecting with this immense love, should be obvious to all aspirants of the Higher Path: we will then, and only then be able to use the interdimensional language-of-the-light, connect with the original Sons of Lyra, bring back the original teachings on how to move creation forward.

80. Lyra – Pleiades – Alcyone – Central Sun Adjustor

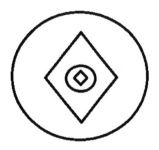

Mary loves this symbol.
This is for Highlighting.
This is good for love
energy.

"This might sound strange, but we [are] writing this book with you."

This symbol is for a "program." As mentioned, highlighting is the awareness program in which we see the separation or the duality of our game. It is a process that occurs within us, as we view the continual blending and movement between structure and free-flowing creation. Duality exists within the smallest parts of ourselves, however, the collective group known as Mary, explains to us that we are simply energy adjustors! Our creative power is never limited, it is forever moving in this now moment.

The Lyra-Pleiades link serves to show us our true selves: magnified units of individuated consciousness, operating through All-loving collectives of consciosness. Our specific programs have been created to experience a shared sense of unity, as love is creation.

81. Lyra- Genetics formatting, Accelerator, Accumulation of Particles

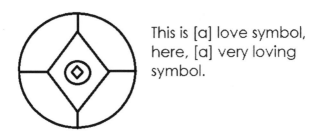

This is [a] love symbol, here, [a] very loving symbol.

This symbol resembles a highlighting symbol with lines.

The next message was for me to write the names of the Lyrans working with me.

1. Entura

2. Emio

3. Eson

4. Emway

5. Emsa

6. Elohim

"Here are some names of friends and others will be shown to you."

Next, they told me that I am a "ley-line opener", and said, "All your Higher Selves [are] working with you. A lot of energy is coming for

75

you."

They then said each of these names twice: "Some names for you, that will be shown, who you are. Releasing."

"Merra; Elohim; Semmol; EnRa; Braa; Dwal; Ur; Tem. [...] Mary; Dwal; Dorian; Semma; Desta; Hella; Merra; Erra."

*When you see a "cross" inside of a circle, it often signifies interdimensional travel taking place.

82. Lyra – Pleiades

"Very good! Mary loves this energy."

This is a high energy frequency adjustor called "Mary's Light Code." It is a signal for the [coming] Kingdom of Heaven. It is embued with light-codes and signatures from many star systems, cooperating. The (light-code frequency adjustment) chant comes in: "Seiaha, Emolā, Seiaha, Emolā, Seiaha, Emolā, Seiaha, Emolā.

Emolā, Emolā, Éiahā, Emolā.

Emolā, Emolā, Éiahā, Emolā.

Emolā, Emolā, Éiahā, Emolā.

Semolā, Semolā, Éiahā, Emolā. Tot."

"The frequencies of Lyra have been adjusted. Phase complete. Thank you."

83. Lyra – Training sequence beings

Gateway Activation Code

Example of activation that came through while viewing this code:

"Sovereign light beings come in with this code. Elohim training device. Opening stargate X44. Sovereign. Leader. Training. Begins. Breakthroughs. Sweet sounds. Lyra. Opening. Stagate. 1218. 1214. 1219. 1245. Sovereign. Light beings. Enter. Light beacons. Only highest in Lyra. Make sounds. Training. Thank you."

84. Lyra – Leadership Activation Symbol a.k.a. Timeship Earth capsule

Lyran
Communicator
"Device"
"expulsion rate 45"

"Uniting four tribes, this sign holds frequency coding for an organic training device, located above Earth. It's frequency changes. Spinning rate of propulsion is not the same as expulsion rate. Expulsion rate is the harmony (sound) generated by the spin rate. Each device records Velatropa (Earth). The sign for this device is in four parts, because the larger part of the device has not yet been recorded. The keepers of the records, maintain that the device will be shown, soon. Message for humanity: create more leaders and more devices will be shown. Sovereign connections must be made. We will change."

Then they said in a long whisper: "Krista, might you know we love you."

85. Pleiades & ATEN – Activation

Harmonious sign for peace-keeping in the Universe.

Specific frequencies have been adjusted throughout this book. You will understand when you connect to the infinite part of who-you-are.

In the "Lyran Training Device" -mechanism, the Lyrans have given us several tidbits about "their" (or our) work.

It is my understanding, that when Lyran leaders are fully activated upon this planet, we will begin to work with extraterrestrial harmonics beyond this plane. Our planet is currently healing at a very fast rate, and these symbols promise to exponentially improve that rate. We hope you enjoyed this journey. (It is also my guess that many of these symbols have or could be used for personal insignias for space-wear.)

Conclusion

The timeship Earth, has created a program in which it has kept itself confined. This means that the timelines associated with Ascension are constantly moving and changing. Why? Because they accumulate knowledge through separation. Now, it is up to us, as luminaries, to bring back several timelines which have been forgotten in the Mass Consciousness program. We explained to Creator that we had a sense of "reoccuring nightmares", in which we were involved in fallen consciousness. It meant that once aware of the Creator's Light, we no longer wanted to play separation that way we did for so long- it was time to being the re-awakening of codes, municipalities, constructs of higher awareness that meant we would all begin to assimilate to a new wavelength.

This new wavelength is in part, being assimilated through the light codes of the light-carriers and those beings who have chosen to awaken the Adamic Seed Coding of 12-strand DNA, including those of the accelerated Adam, or Atum.

Atum-Re, was the fully awakened, charged light-being with infinite potential. It was one of the original light-bearers, with fully awakened senses. The original form would have included: heightened sense perception where adjacent brain hemispheres where light-codes transmissions were on-going; sexual unification, as in, androgeny to the point where he or she would "choose" their sexual experience; the ability to be taken into the Light of Creator upon will; the carrying of multiple star-lineages; constructs of the mind to allow for the advancement of superior technology. This being would be fully embodying the love of the four, if not twelve, directions; have an entire land-mass for free creation unto itself; embody the spirit of the Overself, and have the ability to magnify its experience of the Earth experiment into other reality programs.

Now, the human Mind is what is continually developing, however, it is the Spirit that is needing its place in our society. Once we begin to awaken these light-codes within ourselves, we must be able to place our communication correctly, delegate tasks which are harmonious to our Mother Earth, and relish in the fact that we are Divine, deserving messengers of love, light and experience. All experience is One, however, when we become more of Who-We-Truly-Are, we begin to experience the Collective Mind, the God Mind, the One Overmind with no name. It is in the infinite, that we find ourselves, placing our hands upon our hearts, swearing to ourselves that we will become more than we have been, since the experience of all lifetimes.

The ultimate question is: how many different ways can we say, "I love you"?

Thank you.

~Krista

Caution: After reading this book, you may be activated into your cosmic leadership role.

For further information about these symbols, it is recommended that you look into both Lemurian symbols and Mayan calendar signs, as these should contain similar codings.

Made in the USA
Middletown, DE
17 January 2019